Wildflower Tea

A Poetry Collection

C. Churchill

C Churchill

Also, by C. Churchill:

I am a woman not a Winston

Color Body Feels

Petals of the Moon

On social media:

Instagram @cc_writes

Facebook @cchurchillwrites

Wildflower Tea

A Poetry Collection

C. Churchill

C Churchill

Where do you grow? Is it in the dark?

Where no one is looking?

Is it under stares of fake smiles and hidden successes?

*Is it in the tea poured gently under steam of
conversations and dreams?*

Or is it in the wild?

Alone without guise?

In notebooks and stacks gently reminding yourself

No one is without failure

No one is without words

Where do you grow?

All her wild was put to rest

Under a long hand of darkness

But she remains

A reflection in the cup

Swirling and twirling

Reminding me

There is light among the dark

There are dreams

There is always a poem

Resting beside the worries of yesterday

My wildflower tea.

C Churchill

Wildflower Tea

The Flood

If I were to recall
All the times
I had to be strong
I would surely drown
In this flood of tears

Instead I swim
Some days
By choice
Some days
Because I know nothing else.

just keep swimming

I saw a cardinal
Sweep the sky
Enter boughs
Amidst the fly
He looked at me
And I at him
He appeared to have a familiar grin
I called your name
Hoping you would hear
Because someone once said
To see a cardinal
Means loved ones are near

I called and called
And the cardinal grinned
Such a smirk
I knew you were within
With a wink
And a flutter
You left my heart
Just as you found it

with a wink and a flutter

I forgot my name
For a minute
Forgot the day
For awhile
Where I was
Where I was going
I forgot so very much
After you were gone
But I never forgot
To say I love you

I just hope you can hear me.

I love you

Some will come to tea only
  When the sun is shining
A few will come no matter the weather
  Let them be your anchor.

anchor

C Churchill

One day

The time came sooner than expected

But also felt late

In a whirlwind as only, storms are akin

I found myself on the edge of reason

Contemplating this late season

Why did the fall make me want to spring and the

 Winter cause stargazing?

Where was my soul?

Where was my mind?

Left on the side like dressing on a diet

To be used sparingly or not at all

Some things clutter

And gather dust as we dwell

All I can say is, this is my sweet hell

To be left alone in thought is

A gift and a curse

Depending on the season, rhyme

Or verse

seasons

I invited you to tea

But you didn't hear me

I called every night for a week

No return

Eventually I gave in

Realizing

My heart

Was louder than my voice

My heart

Spoke a language you didn't understand

And my voice

Was lost in translation.

no words necessary

C Churchill

You kept giving me hand grenades

And I thought they were roses

I was building a garden

And you an arsenal

I was careful to plant them well

Soft hands and sunlight

Just enough tears to make it real

All the while

I was avoiding landmines

And you were

Just waiting for me to fall

Completely.

arsenal

My boots are wet and heavy

Jeans flooded halfway up

Rainy Autumn Days

With a chill to my bones

Feeling alive yet fragile

Beyond summer's sun

Winter is peeking through the frost

Morning's dew. Now frozen

With boots heavy

Jeans flooded halfway up

I manage to collect the fallen leaves

Leaves placed in my path

I put them squarely in my pocket

All dirt covered and worn

Hands muddy

Jeans flooded halfway up

Feeling fragile

Yet alive.

flooded

C Churchill

I walk among humans

I watch the leaves change

Hasn't been summer for more than a day

But they are changing

Before my own eyes

Walking faster

Blurred into spines

Until only slender branches remain

Summer is gone in less than a day.

summers end

I thought grownups weren't afraid of anything

I thought their smiles were real

I thought tears were reserved for children

And more than anything

I wanted to fast forward time

Now that I have grown

I see the faces of children

Smiling, crying, fearing, feeling

I would give anything

To be innocent

To be real

To just feel something.

numb

C Churchill

He smiled at me everyday

I never met his gaze

For I had only known smiles

That ended in tears

And I knew one day

He would look the other way.

villain

I never chose

To stop loving me

To stop loving you

I did not choose

 the clouds that now shadow

I did not choose the flood

But here I am drowning

One day I woke without

The rays of the sun

Without the warmth of flesh

One day I woke

With my eyes closed

blind

C Churchill

I couldn't wash you from my hands

Nor my eyes

No matter who I touched

Or how I cried

In the end

We were just a memory

But this heart

Stays muddy

And your footprints

Know this path well

muddy

I lost the cap to my pen
Five poems ago
Now I suppose I will write till I go
To sleep
To work
To hell
To death

Depending on the pen
And the universe
Of what's left

But that is a writer's life
The pen
The universe
Lost caps
Lost minds
Energy lying in wait
Lost in the nick of time

dried ink

C Churchill

Last time
We had laughs
We had tears
We had
 Shoulders
  Hands
  Arms
   Lips

Last time we had each other

last time

Life was perfect

Just

You

Me

And the wildflower tea

Like Romeo and Juliet

A love story

Most have never met

But all stories come to an end

And only some get

A happily ever after.

fairytales

C Churchill

There are things no one tells you
About being a widow
How your breath seems lost
And exhaling hurts just as much as the
inhale
How your heart forms a new ache
With daily tasks
How what you thought was hard before
Now seems like a walk in the park
There are things no one tells you
About being a widow
Because that pain
Never wants to be said
Out loud.

out loud

What if this heart isn't a home?

What if the ravens don't race the moon?

What if all we know

Of love and life

Are just moments upon memories

Chilled glasses of lemonade

Leaves falling silently

Faces in awe of today

Getting us to the next

Next to nothing

Next to hope

Maybe it's the getting

Not the next

Maybe it's the present

Maybe you are already home.

home

All I held dear

Became the past

The fringe

Unfocused

The ghost in the belfry

A history of life

Settled like an ulcer

An ache

Apparent

No matter

How full my belly

ache

I never knew sadness came in colors other than black

things we learn along the way

C Churchill

From wildflowers

To gunshot wounds

My muse

Has always been you

muse

My white picket fences
Have holes to mend
Paint chipping
Scores of splinters
Wait my hands
Wait my blood
Stained white
As winter's silence
Stained but peeling
Layers
See the decades
Where my hands
Resemble theirs
Where they laid first length
Stolen youth
Stolen from me
From you
Yet hands find home
Where blood and splinters
Hold my name
Hold my tears
But never my heart

fences

C Churchill

When life gets heavy

My eyelids do not

Sleeping comes in waves

I can no longer control

Awake at half past one

Then again at half past three

All the while

Counting sheep

Laughing at me

I wonder if the moon

Sees what has become

Of her once sleeping child

The world has undone.

undone

When you have been shattered to pieces

It is hard to see a person

Not holding a hammer,

a view askew

Obligation
Held tight
Like a corset on the eve of August
Never mind the perspire
As long as the smile held true
Or at least in a posture
That didn't sell despair
Like penny candy on the ice cream truck
route
Hold it together
Held together
Either way
The smile
Was suffocating
And I would have given anything
To breathe

posturing

In the distance
You called my soul
Looking for answers
My heart doesn't know
I sit at the waters edge
Feet dangling in
Forgetting where you end
And I begin

the calling

Whisk me away on a cotton-candy dream

Laying in the dappled sun under that old oak tree

Fields of flowers scented in magic

Summer winds fuel our happiness

Suddenly

The weeks fly past

A cold snap comes

This love won't last

For summer is done and

Harvested hearts lay in the fall

Where the seeds of spring will eventually thaw

summer love

The darkness you fear

A mere illusion of mind

See with your heart

Only magic you will find

seeing

C Churchill

I line my glass with cotton

Afraid of spills and clinks

For ice floats free in summer's heat

And clinks are for weddings

Spills for the careless

And I find my line is straight

To the point

Carrying misforgiving as a

Reminder

Of what days can turn into

heat

One day I was walking

To and fro

Apparently, I wander

So much I don't know

That my wander is aimless

Fueled by

Escape

But this path is eerily worn

With all my mistakes

After considering this journey for a moment or two

I decided to leap

Finally, without you

finally

C Churchill

I sliced my wrists on magic candles

Hoping the flames

Would allow rekindle

Maybe this spell of you will go dark

And I can move past

This flood to sparse

For I know not how deep this well

But buckets are no longer enough

Not even close

flames of yesterday

Give me the white lies

Painted in scarlet

Dripping in your desire

I can take it, lashed and ready

My skin is welted from the last loves sin

And healing is a payment I have yet to win

All is fair in love and war

But I cannot help

See the similarities

in love and war

The Magic

The wildflowers have not gone

They are merely sleeping

As you too must rest

For all things wild deserve

The lullaby of the moon

moon song

I wonder if the stars know

How much

I count on them

wishing

C Churchill

I told him of the leaves

Why they dance in summer's sweet grace

Bustling with fairies and glitter

Dancing forever dancing

His eyes wide

Looking up at the sky

Looking up at me

Dancing

On summer's sweet wind

We tell these tales

Weaving magic in the sands of time

He now tells me of the dancing

Sweet winds gone to years

Floating by

to believe in magic

Oh, the dreamers dally on

The sight of ancients playing to muses

The view of futures for many

In the timeless and infinite stories

Of morality we sing high on happily ever after

Eyes wide searching

Many are open

But blind to reality

They will remain in jest

For hope holds in the blinders

Of once-drawn carriages

Glass slippers

And the stroke of midnight

dreamers

C Churchill

Wild hearts

Find a home

In every place

They roam

roam

This warm breeze

Filled with melancholy and fresh tea

Keeps me dreaming

Of what could be

I see a cloud

It speaks your name

In hearts and wonder

I am to blame

A keeper of stars

Lying under a blanket

Wishing

This warm breeze

Filled with melancholy and fresh tea

Keeps me dreaming

Of what could be

melancholy and fresh tea

C Churchill

As long as I can remember

There have been rumors

Rumors of women, of witches, of gifts

Of rushed phone calls, whispers in the dark

All my life

I have felt this pull

Towards something greater

something powerful, something familiar

Today I planted myself in the deepest wood

Among the ancient trees

With soil unturned for centuries

Today I let the earth bring me home

So, I could be born again

Into legacy

Into magic

women of magic

Just a girl I was

Never shown the way

Pushed down stairs

Landing flat on my face

I reeled and rallied

And tried my best

But the universe

Had other plans

For my pink dress

The boys they looked

But never swallowed

There was no hook, line and sinker

For this wildflower

Just a girl I was

Never shown the way

I am forever grateful

For landing flat on my face

For when I looked up

The stars were ready

Welcoming me

As wild

No dress necessary

pink dress

C Churchill

Fairytales breathe

Life into me

Meadows fresh

Of dragon's breath

Sun burns while the moon storms

Every turn

A star is born

I choose to believe

In magic you see

For incredible things

Have happened to me

And I wont dismay over the darkness

I will turn the page again

For all things have balance

And this chapter is yet to end.

chapters

Sometimes our hearts

Need to visit

The dark

To see that we are

Full of light

hope

C Churchill

I sit most mornings

Coffee in hand

Kittens curled

Only after screams

Lead to bellies full

Peace

Has come

Finally

Six hours after waking

Three thirty-three

Tends to be

My witching hour

Where I wake

Abrupt

As if explosives

Were beneath me

Holding my tongue

No breathe escaping

My witching hour

But a quarter of a day later

I can breathe

And the coffee in my mug

Fills my veins and

Silences the ghosts

A moment of peace

Mine for the taking

peace of mine

C Churchill

Forgotten but not lost

I rose to my feet

Determined to survive

I would be no damsel in distress

Insecurity would not best me

I wasn't the ugly duckling you branded

Nor anyone's swan song

But an eagle

Preparing to fly

fly

I have sat for hours

In a place time forgot

Untouched by eyes and hands

Once all over me

Now I sit

Not afraid

Even though alone

For hours

For days

Unafraid

Free.

free

C Churchill

Some days

We pick up the pieces

Other days

We throw them to the sky

Hoping the moon

Will carry us

With the other stars

That have died

stars

In the meadows

I find myself

Staring into the sun

Such a sinful girl I am

Going blind just to feel the light

Pierce deep

Peirce long

Pierce anywhere I don't belong

For this meadow

This sun

This day I go blind

Is a fair trade barter

To release my shadow

From this prison I call home

shadow

C Churchill

For as many times as you

Called my name

The Wild always

Called my soul

the wild

Although the path

Is sometimes camouflaged

We proceed

Feeling our way

With intuition

And a touch

Of madness

madness

When you

Are holding stars

In your eyes

Hiding in the dark

Will never

Be an option

hiding

I always loved the storm of a fresh June sky

For what could be more wonderful

   Than the moon crying

      Just before the rise

storm

C Churchill

Some days

The chains are heavy

 Some days

They give me

Just enough room

To dream

and I will

I am all good

And all evil

I am moon

And yet wolf

I hunger

I feed

I feast

I am free

I howl

I shine

I run

I hide

I am the echo of last night's dream

Haunting and loving

In the same scream

I am all good

And all evil

I am moon

And yet

I am wolf

I am wolf

C Churchill

In the hour between darkest dark
And blinding bright
I have fallen off maps
and been caught in flight
No worries to speak at the wee hour of 4:33
Just a long list of don't give-a-fucks
Hot coffee and me
I am an early bird
Always chasing the worm
The one that eludes me when conversations been stirred
I need a moment
Some time to myself
To sort through these pages
Hot coffee and wealth
For I am rich
With dreams and wonder
Seemingly stifled
When the world comes to grumble
I am an early bird
Forgive me today
For I am not available for fucks
Only dreams
And flying away.

no fucks

Wildflowers
Are not jealous of the rose
They are not manicured just so
They breathe free
No worry of thorns
They are not picky, never scorned
They don't end up in the trash
After a lover's promises
Are taken back
Wildflowers are free of vain
Free to dance
Free to remain

Wild

never a rose

You can pull me apart
Petal by petal
But in the end
I will hold the
Seeds
And you will hold
The love me nots

in the end

Finding magic in the dark
Is never as easy as it may seem
But if you trust your heart
All things are possible

possible

C Churchill

Of all the wild

The trails untethered

All the nights

Storms weathered

We still manage

To make it to this place

A place to bloom again

Despite this hectic race

life

Took a trip down memory lane

It was what I expected

I have changed

I outgrew this place long ago

Time to be moving on

As I continue to grow

changed

C Churchill

I embrace every tear that falls

Because it took a long time

To feel

Anything

At all

embrace

The day teased me with desires of the norm

Albeit I had heard of these daydreams

Of nine to fives and matching curtains

I never once had them

Or seen many in my life

Matching curtains were a dream

When sheets were off color and

And days were laid off

I could never quite grasp the cleaver in the beaver

Or vice versa

Of dinner on the table by five thirty-two

Or clothes ironed and put away

I just tend to file these things under

Daydreams and fables

And other things we think about

When our grass has gone brown again

always greener

C Churchill

Butterflies are only

Fragile when

They forget

They can

Fly

fragile

There is magic in this blood

The letting has occurred

I still wait at heavens gate

Even though the angels no longer sing

And my praise has lost its tune

But this magic still courses

And I have yet to see

Why the magic

Has in fact

Chosen me

half heartedly

C Churchill

Lavender crickets

Chime in tune

Of forgotten suns

And harvested moons

We lie speechless as the world comes to order

In a slumber be it

Begged, borrowed or stolen

Awaiting a wave of sweet peace and peonies

To grace our still bodies

With understood larceny

For the balance is giving and taking and weight

Sleeping lids providing much needed faith

We still at the thought of being raped

By something so magical and indeed

So great

That we give more than we can and release those

Inhibitions

Proper and skilled

To every passing magician

magic and other vices

The bloom will happen

When we are fully tended

ready

The Bloom

Water me gently my love

Delicate touches

Make me bloom

touching

Can you tell me what it is like?

To see in the rain

Sing with the birds

Release this pain

Can you tell me what it is like?

To feel love drown you in one breath

And break cages in the very next

Flying without purpose

Landing without regret

Can you tell me if it's you?

The one to show me the way

Can you tell me if this love is true?

Before I give my heart away

can you

These bones ache

Like the dust- covered scrolls

Of old proverbs and timeless quotes

Early to bed

Early to rise

Through life

True love

True lies

Where we can't find peace and we know no rest

We return to the words that we love the best

words

I have been searching for a way to fill this heart

That doesn't mean I don't love

It doesn't mean I can't love

It just means I know how to love so deep

That my heart extends far beyond my soul

Into the deepest dark

Finding the very stars, you seek

found

I survive on broken wings

Learning to fly on a curve

Life handed me challenges

And I met them with adventure

Embracing the diversity within

Only took my instincts higher

Flying above my brokenness

Making happiness rain from my storm

rain

Whenever

I feel like I am

Drowning

The sun reminds me

I am only growing

And that

In fact

May take my breath away

growing

C Churchill

There are times

The world just seeps

Into you

Those are my favorite

submerged

I love the fragrant scent of life

The one that fills me

When you fill me

With hope

With love

With what can become

fragrant

C Churchill

You looked into me so deeply

A mirror emerged

The me looking back

Was new

Even to myself

new

Too many times

We falter for the fall

What if we tip toe

This time

And perhaps

We will find grace

Instead of

Skinned knees

skinned knees

C Churchill

You held my hand

Not to lead

Not to scold

But only to be there

You held my hand

At the same level

As my heart

uncommon

I gain clarity

In the forest deep

A sense of wisdom

Not found on a city street

Maybe it's the shadows

That whisper folks and lore

Maybe it's the quiet

Nothing more

quiet wisdom

I return to her

The glades sweeping

She calls on me

Her wildflower

Her my muse

We sit hours in silence

Communicating the breeze

As the sun clouds in patterns, both at ease

I return to her

The glades weeping

For now, it's been so long

She calls more softly now

Wildflower?

Yes, my muse

I am here

I have forgotten to visit this past year

With life as I know it ripped from my hoist

I am barely afloat on this strange course

Here I am today

To sit in the breeze

Not to tell of my year's past

But to remember life

Before this crash

before the crash

C Churchill

They know my name

Not much else

They know my past

Not much else

They know my words

But not my lies

Not my heart

Not my guise

They know my name

Not much else

For they are only they

They are

Not you.

never you

I am the spring

A bit chilly to hold

I am the bud

Newly formed

I am spindly branches

Heavy with dew

I am me

In skies of blue

I sleep in nooks of old oaks and nest with Robin eggs

For my season is spring

Amidst awkward wobble legs

Of lambs and colts too new to see

That spring holds more magic

Than we will ever see

For bloom and bough have ribbons adorned

Like gifts from heavy pockets

Raining April storms

I am spring

Newly formed

spring

C Churchill

I used to sit for hours

The mirror my guide

Showing me how to primp and prune

How to be my best

How to survive

In a world of endless filters on faces

Souls are lost in these strange places

Accommodating to say the least

Compliant at every turn

We primp, we prune

We accommodate

Till we are blue

Never enough in this strange place

I broke my mirror

Before I lost my faith

filters

I am rubber you are glue

I tell myself these words you choose

Could break me a thousand different ways

If I let them

If I stay

So, I pack my rubber boots and gloves

Heading away from our "love sweet love"

I don't know where I will go

But I am aware you are not my home

For home is a place you feel safe

Not a battle to save face

rubber and glue

C Churchill

I spilled more than tea

The day you kissed me

I didn't expect to fall in love

Nor this poetry

But words found a place I never have known

Fitting just right

Like the tea that first morning

kissed right

swift foxes

lazy days

blooms aplenty

fill displays

lovers ready

rabbits play

we all need some fun

amidst the grey

play with me

C Churchill

Quit sweeping your magic

under the rug

All things magical

are a little messy

messy

It took a minute

A somewhat long minute

I never knew where I would go

Or how I would grow

I planted myself

 in the wisdom of time

Healing as I went

suffering the crime

I have lived many stories

in many lives

 Been cut down

  by various knives

But here I am

blooming again

A slightly different shade

than before I began

shades of time

No matter where you are in your healing

You can always take a breath

Just a moment

To see how far you have come

Indulge in your process

You are worth a breath or a few

just breathe

I spent timeless moments

Thinking of what will be

Wasted sand

Drowning me

Wishing I could find my two left feet

For at least they could transport me

To another time?

No, not really

But moving forward is a reality

We all need a boost

Here and there

And if I could share anything

It would be

You are the one to take you there

one step at a time

C Churchill

I have gotten ink upon this sleeve

The one that my heart beats free

It doesn't matter if they can see

Because all I ever wanted

Was to be me

just being me

One thing I know for certain

Is the tide is ruled by the moon

Not unlike me

Not unlike you

In a world of missed connections

We are all so very connected

We beat to a different drum

But at the same time, we are all beating

We are all breathing

We are all living

Under the same moon

Experiencing tides

tides

C Churchill

It might just be time

To dust off your crown

You have lived in penance long enough

Sit tall my friend

This life is far from over

And royalty is in the eye of the beholder

you are worthy

Sometimes we lose
That one person
The one person that knew
Our heart
Our soul
Our dreams and wishes
They are still here
Just not the way we planned
But once you have a connection
It is everlasting

for KK

C Churchill

You have fought so long

You have loved even longer

Never forget that

Never forget you are so much more than your
past

for Sarah

There is a sisterhood

That resides

When pain is our demise

We claim refuge among hearts

That feel this pain

But we also lend to magic

And in that we find family

We find sisters

We find hope

for Tiffany

C Churchill

There is love

Where we least expect it

And connection

In friends we have not met

But I see real

In places I have yet to travel

I see love

Among the kindred

I see you

for Saide

We are all wildflowers

Free to grow

As we please

If we keep the shadows at bay

We can bloom

just bloom

C Churchill

I have seen the devil in the pale moon light

I have danced with all my foes

I have been breathing to survive

Longer than I know

If per chance

There is one last breath

To say I love you

I will always use it

swan song

I haven't had the easiest path

I have been dared to survive

That is when others look at you

And wonder how you are still alive

Because folks they know have been through much less

And lost their minds at the first digress

I can't say I am winning but I can say I am here

I am trying with every breath to survive every year

I may not be successful but at least I have my voice

Which hasn't been stifled yet

Give me a moment

I will catch a flame

I will burn brighter than you have ever seen

burn brighter

C Churchill

Thank you all so very much.

C Churchill

Index

About the author

Churchill currently resides in Michigan. Recently she received her MA in Secondary Education. She spends her time writing and creating art. You can find her artwork as well as signed copies of her books for sale on her Etsy shop

C Churchill Poetry.

Books by C. Churchill

Petals of the Moon

Wildflower Tea

Color Body Feels

I am a woman not a Winston

Never stop searching for yourself